A Pocket of Coins

Your Guide to Positive Living

Donna Baird, Ph.D.

Foreword

We all get "stuck" in our lives at some time or another. Those of us who are successful or happy, happen to discover ways to get "unstuck". The following book is about how Dr. Baird, drawing on her clinical skills and applying them to her own life experiences attained success and personal happiness. It is easy to read but draws on concepts that have been shown to be effective for a number of others throughout the years. The experience for Dr. Baird came from personal experience and an "Ah Ha" moment. The result is a very usable manual for personal growth.

Dr. William B. Lawson,MD, PhD. DFA.P.A.

Preface

The ideas in this book have been buzzing around as abstractions in my head for some time now. Finally, I decided to sit down and put them on paper in the form of a short inspirational guide.

The whole idea began when, some time ago, I was having a particularly stressful day and the sincerity of my actions was questioned by someone dear to me. The circumstance challenged me to take an honest and critical look at myself. This snowballed into a period of introspection, self-evaluation and action in which I sought to gain deeper insight into my "true self": the person I am now, compared to the person I want to become.

Each insight opened up new areas of my life that needed work and attention. I decided that I was worth the investment of time and energy, so I did the hard work and I learned a lot about myself. What I discovered made a profound difference in my life. It involved a process of purging old beliefs and attitudes as well as reaffirming and reshaping my life. During the process I learned many principles that I have discovered to be timeless and universal. I learned them the hard way - first-hand - so I know they work. And I want share these simple processes with you.

The title, "A Pocket of Coins," came to me quite spontaneously. I thought it a fitting title as it captured just what I intended this book to offer -- a shared experience. Very often, just when we feel close to giving up, along comes a just-in-time smile, a word of encouragement, a thought or a touch. I think of these as "life coins". I sincerely hope this little pocket of coins finds its way into your hands at a time when you need it most.

We all have a few coins in our pockets -- we share them each time we help someone in need.   It's the little extra of ourselves that we give to others.   It's part of our continuous striving toward true humanness… toward living fully, boldly and authentically.   This book is just my way of sharing a few coins I've picked up along my way.

In this guide we will look, very briefly, at ten principles or processes.   We will actively engage in each process by doing and committing.   I encourage you to tackle one process at a time.   This allows you to clearly pinpoint the impact that particular process is having on your life.   Most important, be sure to share what you've learned with others.   It is only in a dynamic exchange with loved ones that any new principle really takes root in our lives.

So...to all who have shared your coins with me over the years, thank you, thank you.   I hope, in some small way, this little coin collection returns the favor.

Acknowledgements

I want to thank my family, the Baird Klan for all your support. Thanks to Andrew Wolfendon, a true editor. Also, thanks to all my friends who encouraged me in my pursuits and whose lives have brought meaning to mine.

I dedicate this book to
those persons who are in a continual
search for
meaning in their lives.

Contents

Purging

It's impossible to start a process of recovery without a sound knowledge of what you're recovering from.   You must be honest with yourself about yourself.   The first step in this process is to truly understand that it is okay to be imperfect.   It's okay to admit that your behavior is, at times, selfish, rude, needy, and even hateful.   You must give yourself permission to be completely honest about your own "flaws."   Remember: owning your shortcomings can't hurt you (only failing to own them can hurt!).

Understanding that these "negative" traits and behaviors often hurt you more than the person you're targeting should help you to commit yourself to changing them.

And, so today you will seize the opportunity to purge yourself of many of the so-called negative traits and behaviors you've been carrying around and repeating in your life. This will require setting aside an entire day to be alone and reflect on yourself.   Why? Because you're worth it!

Think of this as a true mental health day. Not the kind of casual mental health day we take just to get away from the stresses of everyday life.   No.   This is a day specifically designed to gain deeper knowledge of yourself and begin the process of moving on from negative habits you may have carried your entire life.

So don't tackle this step until you're ready to invest some real time and attention in it. Okay?

When you're ready, then, what I would like you to do is go to a place where you feel safe and comfortable and where you can spend some quiet time alone without interruptions.   Light some candles or put on some meditative music if it helps.   Then I would like you to take some time to think deeply about all the qualities in yourself that you consider "negative."   You know what they are; you probably just don't

enjoy thinking about them very much. Why?
Well, because thinking about
"negative"perceptions of ourselves brings up
some very uncomfortable feelings.   And that's
why we avoid facing them directly.

But understand this: it is our very reluctance to
feel the feelings associated with our "negative"
self-assessments that keeps us stuck in them
and prevents us from moving on.   So, we're
going to do a four-step process.   We're going
to: 1) identify our negative behaviors and
patterns on paper, 2) deeply and fully feel the
feelings attached to them, 3) completely
accept these feelings with an attitude of pure
self-love, and 4) commit to some new
behaviors and approaches.

Ready?

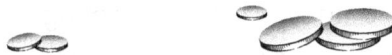

1. Okay. Write a list of those persistent
behaviors and traits that you feel create a
negative you. (Yes, even that one).   Be
honest. No one is going to see this list but you.

2. Now go through the list, one item at a time,
and for each of these "negatives," feel

Whatever feelings come up. You'll surely feel some discomfort and this might seem scary and "dangerous" at first.   But know this: your feelings, no matter how powerful, can't kill you or even harm you.   It is only our erroneous belief that feelings can harm us that prevents us from fully feeling them and moving through them.

As you feel each feeling, remove all mental labels and judgments from it.   Strip the feeling of whatever name you usually give it; just feel it in your body as raw energy.   When you do this, you will realize that emotions are neither positive nor negative; they are simply forms of energy.   Even pain is not actually "bad" when we stop thinking of it as a negative.   Studies have shown that the feelings we call excitement produce the exact same physiological changes as the feelings we call fear.   We just interpret one emotion as positive, the other negative, depending on the circumstances.

Stripped of interpretations and judgments, our feelings lose their power to scare us.   In fact, when we simply "have" our feelings without

4

repressing, labeling or judging them, we realize that all feelings are essentially "positive": that is, they are all expressions of the fundamental life energy that flows through us and makes us alive.   Some call this energy love.

3. Once you have gotten to a place where you can feel your feeling in your body without labeling it mentally, then accept it thoroughly and send it love.   Yes, love.   Love the feeling. Now, love yourself for having the feeling.   Can you do that?   Great!

4. After you have felt, accepted and loved the feeling that comes up for each negative behavior or trait on your list, cross it out and turn it into a positive.   For example, a habit of speaking critically to your family members might be replaced by a commitment to express love and appreciation for them instead.

You've now begun the process to a new you!

You may also want to physically purge yourself as part of your inner purging process.   This is a great idea that will really help all your new changes take root.   There are many healthy physical cleansing options available – you can check with your doctor for a recommendation.   Purging is enhanced when we make it a both a physical and a spiritual experience.

vOf course, let's be real here.   Eliminating the negatives in the above way is not the total cure.   The total cure comes when you intentionally live out positive behaviors in your daily life.   Will people still hurt you? Yes!   Will you still feel depressed at times? Yes!   The difference, however, is that you will now be healthier in your mind and body.   Your emotional and spiritual immune system will be better equipped to withstand and overcome the external stressors, because you are being intentional about living in a positive place…daily.   Remember: all your power is within!

Negatives to purge   Turned into a Positive

_____

_____

_____

Acceptance

The next powerful step you can take toward
creating a thriving life of joy is to fully accept
yourself and every single person, object,
circumstance and past event in your life.
Completely and without judgment or
reservation.

Yes.   Accept every single part of your life
without exception.

We human beings are the only creatures on
Earth who practice the art of non-acceptance.
Not coincidentally, we are also the only
creatures on Earth capable of living in
perpetual misery.   We seem to believe, deep
down, that the way to change something we
think is wrong, unwanted, or substandard is to
reject it - to say, "This I refuse to accept." It's
as if we think, deep down, that this will moment,

somehow make the unwanted condition go away.   Or change it.

Conversely, we think that to accept something means to give it our seal of approval.   We don't want to do that with "negative" things.   So we go about in a constant state of non-acceptance.

But this is flawed thinking.   Acceptance does not mean approval or endorsement.   It just means non-judgmentally and non-emotionally acknowledging something as real.   The fact is, whatever is, is.   If there's a boulder in your living room, there's a boulder in your living room.   You cannot change the world in this moment, nor is it your job to do so.   The world is perfect as it is.   Even in its imperfections.

Non-acceptance is actually the ultimate act of arrogance.   When we refuse to accept the world exactly as it is, we're saying to the Creator, in effect, "You screwed up – I could do a better job of running the universe than You."

Our refusal to accept reality does not aid us in making the world and our own lives a better place. Rather, it actively prevents us from doing do.

Why? Because we can only move on from a place that we accept and acknowledge. It's like using a map when we're lost.   If we don't accept the fact that we're lost and take careful note of where we are right now, we can never get to where we want to be.

How can you move forward from a place you refuse to accept?

Accept yourself and everything about your life. So what if you don't have the biggest house, the nicest car, or the most fashionable clothes. Live anyway!   Non-acceptance is our biggest source of unhappiness and depression.   It places our ability to be happy on something external, something outside of ourselves.   It allows us to blame our husbands or partners, our job or our children for our unhappiness.

The fact is, our happiness originates within.   It is a free choice. We can choose to be happy, regardless of our present circumstances.
Just as we can choose to be miserable in the lap of luxury.

There are blissfully happy prisoners of war; there are miserable hotel heiresses.

Happiness starts with accepting what is. Try it. Just simply say, "It is not my job to run the universe. I cannot force the world, in this moment, to be different. Therefore, I fully accept everything exactly as it is."

The moment you truly accept what is, you will feel a tremendous weight fly off your shoulders and the potential for happiness will begin.

In order to help yourself accept those things you consider "negative," you can do a version of the exercise I gave you for Purging. That is,
1) think about the person, event, thing or circumstance you're having trouble accepting,
2) feel the feelings that come up for you,
3) strip those feelings of any labels, names or judgments and just experience their raw energy,
4) accept those feelings, send them love and send love to yourself for feeling them,
5) make a statement of positive acceptance about the person, event, thing or circumstance.

It's that simple! (Not necessarily easy, but simple).

Some time ago, I spoke with a woman who'd had a three-year "secret" affair with the pastor of her church.   During the entire course of the affair, she'd been hoping that he would leave his wife.   When he finally told her that he would not leave his wife; she was devastated and hopeless.   She refused to accept the reality of what had happened.   She overdosed on pills.

Some time later she disclosed the relationship to a friend, who confessed to her that she had also had a three-year relationship with the same pastor.   He'd done the same thing to her friend!   At this point the woman had no choice but to accept the situation and even to laugh about it.   What a fool she had been! It was only in her acceptance that she was able to start loving herself again.

Self-love is vital to acceptance. We all need a hug sometimes.   So learn to give self-hugs. Yes!   Wrap your arms around your neck and shoulders hang on tight.   Now you're loving you.

Acceptance does not mean that your work is done, though – it has only just begun.   But acceptance is a wonderful and magical starting place.

I will accept the following people, conditions, events and circumstances that I have been refusing to accept:

_____

_____

_____

_____

_____

_____

_____

_____

_____

_____

_____

_____

_____

_____

_____

_____

Begin (take some action steps)

Now that you've learned more about yourself, and you've started to accept yourself and the circumstances of your life, you're ready to make some changes.   You're ready to add action to the process.

Change seems like such a daunting and scary prospect that we often become paralyzed into inaction.   We don't want to give up our old ways all at once!   But it's helpful to remind ourselves that we don't have to change everything about our lives, today, in one moment.   No, we only need to begin.   To take that first step.

After that first step, reality shifts, new possibilities arise and the best next step presents itself.   That's how change happens; step by step.   Not all at once.

I've always loved this quote, usually attributed to Goethe:

"Concerning all acts of initiative (and creation), there is one elementary truth, the ignorance of which kills countless ideas and splendid plans: that the moment one definitely commits oneself, then Providence moves too. All sorts of things occur to help one that would never otherwise have occurred. A whole stream of events issues from the decision, raising in one's favor all manner of unforeseen incidents and meetings and material assistance, which no man could have dreamed would have come his way. Whatever you can do, or dream you can do, begin it. Boldness has genius, power, and magic in it. Begin it now."

There is no time like the present to stop blaming others for your circumstances and to take that crucial first step.   If you're overweight, start researching diet and exercise plans.   If you need a job or you need to change jobs, start looking at online career sites.   If you want to go back to school, register for classes.   If you want to repair a relationship, sit down and write an email or pick up the phone.

Begin.   Until you take an action step, all of your beautiful intention lies bound up in unrealized potential.   None of its power is actualized.   The moment you act, you unleash your intention into the world and "Providence moves too."

True, you can hold onto hurt and use that as an excuse not to act.   But what good does that do you?   The only person you "punish" is yourself.

As you think about changing some aspect of your life, are you worried about what others might think? Is that what's holding you back? Well, it's true - some people will compliment you for your changes, others won't.   Some will support you, some will create obstacles. But either way, it's their issue, not yours.   All you can do is take care of your own business and let the cards fall where they will.

Many of us cling to stasis.   We want predictability.   We want today to feel like yesterday.   I tell clients that something is wrong in your life if you always remain the same.   It means there is no growth.   The truth is, the power within you will give you whatever you need to keep moving forward. You just need to start.

Today.

Make that leap of faith and the higher ground you seek will bow down to cradle your feet.

This is no time for complacency /procrastination. In the world or in our personal lives.   Barack Obama ran his campaign for the presidency on change and won.   How about you waging a personal campaign built on positive change?

There is more to fear in not changing than there is in change.

Change provides you with opportunities to become all you can be.   To tap your unlimited potential. To venture into uncharted paths.

To unburden yourself of the heavy weight of old habits .

Let's release fear together and welcome change!

I will take the following beginning steps this week:

_____

_____

_____

_____

_____

_____

_____

_____

_____

_____

_____

_____

_____

_____

_____

_____

Forgiveness

At some point, we have to make the conscious decision to let go of hurts and pains – we have to forgive.   It's amazing how much control and power we allow others to have in our lives.   That's exactly what we're up to when we cling to blame and anger We're relinquishing the power to create our own happiness and putting that power in the hands of those who have "offended" us.   In a sense, we're allowing the "offender" to hurt us over and over again, on a daily basis.   We're giving them a blank check to make us miserable. In perpetuity.

I remember being utterly trapped in feelings of disappointment and hurt by people in my life. Every day I would dwell on how such "bad" things could happen to me when I am a "good" person.   I would fixate on these feelings so

much that they started to consumo my life.   I
literally felt sick.

I've talked with family, friends and clients
who've gone through tough times and many of
them have felt the same way.   Whether they
suffered because of a broken relationship, a
broken promise, or even a violent or criminal
act, they put their lives on hold for months or
years as they wallowed in blame and anger.

In my case, I decided that I had to let go of the
hurt and anger.   But simply telling myself to let
go did not achieve the ultimate goal because,
as we all know, the mind doesn't simply forget.

No, in order to move on, I had to truly forgive.
Forgive my nemesis.   Yes, we have to release
the negative energies we're holding toward
the person who has caused us deep and
lasting pain.   It is not easy.

From a Young Woman Struggling with Forgiving her Mother

I've hated my mother for most of my life. I never did anything to her, but she just hates me for some reason. About a year ago, her actions led to my daughter being taken away from me. Mother's day 2007, I planned to strangle her, and then turn myself in. Turns out that things didn't go as I planned, and I ended up in a psych hospital.

Over the years, I started to use drugs, which made my problems even worse. I've since lost touch with my daughter, who was the most important person to me.

I'm now talking about these things with my therapist, but I don't think I could ever forgive my mother.

We have to be willing to give up our victim status. And often we have begun to identify with that status so we don't want to let go of it.

We have to say, "I'm no longer willing to live a life of entrapment by hurt and anger."

Forgiveness is not the same as forgetting
Nor is it the same as approval. When we
forgive someone for causing us harm, we are
not saying, "I'm okay with what you did." What
we are saying is that we release the emotional
hold that person or event has on our lives. We
release the blame and the bitterness. Not for
the sake of the other person, but for our own
sake.

Forgiveness is really just another form of
acceptance. It means saying, "I accept that
this thing happened to me - because it did -
and I am ready to move on." I choose to live
in love and freedom rather than bitterness and
immobility.

Sometimes we ourselves are the ones most
needing forgiveness. Sometimes we are the
ones who may have caused disappointment
and pain for others. Learning to forgive
ourselves can be even more challenging than
forgiving others because we have to be willing
to admit that we erred. This is very difficult

for most of us.   We all want to think of ourselves as "good" people.   Somewhere deep inside we believe that "bad things happen to bad people and good things happen to good people".   The truth is: good and bad things happen to all of us at some point in our lives.   Some of it we can control and some of it we can't.

But what we can always control is our ability to let go.   Some of us may need the help of therapy or counseling to do this.   That's okay. Don't be afraid to seek that help.   There is no purpose to a life suffocated by hurt and pain. None whatsoever.   You are no help to yourself or to others as long as you cling to blame and bitterness.

Only you possess the key to your own liberation.   You can rise above even the most unthinkable of offenses if you have the courage to forgive.

So take an hour or so today to carefully review your life.   Think about all those people and events that you blame for causing you pain

and stuckness and write them down below.
Then, for each one (whether a person, an
event or a thing), say, "I release you of all the
power I have given you to bring pain and
suffering into my life.   Regardless of what
you may or may not have done to me, I accept
all responsibility for having created my own
pain.   I forgive you completely and send you
love."

People, events and behaviors I choose to
forgive:

_____

_____

_____

_____

_____

_____

_____

_____

_____

_____

_____

_____

Kindness

Forgiveness is crucial to moving forward in our lives.   But if we really want to drink the nectar of human relationships and raise our lives to a higher level, we need to practice kindness. And we need to do it often.

One of the simplest and most powerful ways to immediately start living a more rewarding life – I mean today, right this very minute – is to be kind to others.   This is one of the greatest feelings of fulfillment we can experience. Kindness is the key by which universal Love flows into our lives.

I recently saw the finale of Oprah's "Big Give" show.   I was so thrilled about the winner. He displayed a kindness and willingness of spirit that was incredibly warm and embracing.   He was big enough to follow through with his idea for helping inner city kids, but he was just as enthusiastic about his competitor's idea and worked just as tirelessly to make that idea a success.

I remember years ago, I myself had a burning desire to take a group of young people from inner city New York to Washington, DC.   Most of them had never been out of their neighborhood.   I wanted them to visit their nation's capital, not just see it on television.

It seemed that everything and everyone put barriers in my way, but I persisted even when it meant that someone else would get the credit. Because it wasn't about me--it was about the kids.

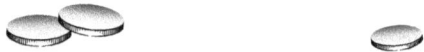

At the end of the excursion, one boy decided that he wanted to attend college at a university in Washington, DC.   And I was most touched when one young girl came up to me and asked if I would adopt her.   This was her expression of appreciation for the experience.

There is such utter satisfaction in giving to and helping others, whether they are less fortunate than us or more so. Some would say that there is even a "high" you get by giving and practicing kindness. Your spirit is buoyed up, the impossible seems possible and you feel as if you can accomplish anything.

One of the great mysteries of human life is why we are so stingy with our kindness. Despite the fact that every time we give lovingly of ourselves we feel a thousand percent better, we still seem to cling to the idea that giving represents a loss or a cost of some kind. It doesn't, of course. It is a gain/gain proposition. Both we and the person receiving the kindness benefit immensely from the exchange.

> A Man's Willingness to be Kind
>
> My wife was hesitant when her cousin called to ask if
> we could take in a young lady who was a victim of a
> violent crime.   This person was attacked during a
> visit home from university.   One of her hands was
> severed at the elbow and the other was so severely
> maimed, she had only about a 10% use of it.
> Although we did not know her, her circumstance
> sounded so desperate that we felt compelled to help.
> My family ended up caring of her for almost a year.

On the other hand, each time we stifle the
impulse to be kind, it's a lose/lose deal.

Kindness does not have to cost us money.
We can offer a listening ear, assistance with a
task, or just a kind word or a compliment.   Any
kindness we offer, at any time and to anyone,
adds to the "love quotient" of humanity and
makes the world a better place. It does.
Believe it.

Certainly, the people we love the most should
be the most frequent recipients of our

kindness.   (So many marriages and families go sour simply because people latch onto resentment and forget to simply be kind.)   But "random acts of kindness" are extremely powerful, too.   I know of a wealthy man who carries a roll of hundred-dollar bills in his pocket.   Several times a day, he gives $100 away to an unsuspecting stranger.   Each time he does it, he feels a rush of warmth inside and considers it a gift to himself.

The most important thing to remember about true kindness is that it must be offered without expectations.   It's not a quid pro quo deal. It's a one-way street.   If we offer kindness with any expectation that our gift will be returned to us in the form of a thank-you, appreciation or a returned favor, then what we're offering isn't really kindness.   It's horse trading.   Kindness should be offered because we want to offer it; not because we expect something in return.

Try it.   Today.   Do something for someone. Anyone. Just because...

Today I will show kindness to:

The Art of Non-Doing

We have all heard about the harmful effects of stress. While a manageable level of stress can serve as an impetus for progress, higher levels of stress, as well as chronic stress, can impede our functioning. Stress can be disruptive and can wreck havoc on our state of mind and on our lives. I've seen people grow depressed, suffer from anxiety, and even become destructive to themselves and their loved ones because they're not able to cope with stressors in their lives.

Often times, just having some quiet time to organize our thoughts – or, better still, to not think at all - and just close out the noise of life can be transforming.

Relaxing and meditation are two practices that can enrich our lives inestimably and help us

maintain good mental health as we tackle
challenging changes in our lives.

How do you relax?   Simple.   Take time each
day or at least once a week to just pamper and
show love to yourself.   Get a massage, run a
warm bubble bath with aromatic oils, burn
some incense, oil, or fragrant candle, spray
your favorite perfume, listen to soft music, dim
the lights.   Boy, have I just set the mood here!
Doesn't it feel good just thinking about it?
Envision relaxation, and you can literally feel
your mind and body moving into that mode.

Meditation is another tool that has
incalculable mental and physical health
benefits.   The idea of meditation may sound
"Eastern" or "New Age" to some, but it's really
the most basic practice a human being can do,
other than breathing.   It is not religious in
nature and it does not require any particular
belief systems.   People from all religious
backgrounds practice meditation.

To meditate means simply to set aside some
time every day to sit in silence and stillness

and to let the mind quiet down. Meditation, in essence, is the art of not thinking. As we practice meditation we become more and more adept at allowing our ceaseless stream of thoughts to slow down and stop. We become aware of the silent "bed of awareness" against which thinking takes place.

Many westerners believe that thought is the most basic form of awareness ("I think, therefore, I am."). Meditation shows us this is not the case. It allows us to become aware of the deeper level of consciousness that is aware that we are thinking, that watches our thoughts. This is sometimes called the Witnessing Consciousness. Becoming one with the witness within us is one of the most healing practices known to man.

In study after study, meditation has proven to be an astonishingly effective way to reduce stress. But those who meditate regularly know that this is just the tip of the iceberg. The real benefits of meditation go much further than stress-reduction. They include:

tapping into our deepest levels of wisdom, opening the door to spirit, and triggering spontaneous insights of life-changing magnitude.

Don't hold back.   Treat yourself to a day or evening of sheer pleasure -- relax, you're worth it!   And spend some time each day soaking in precious silence.

This week, to step out of the stress-stream and treat myself with loving care, I will:

_____

_____

_____

_____

_____

_____

_____

_____

_____

_____

_____

_____

Patience

We've all heard the old adage, "patience is a virtue."   On one hand we value patience, but on the other, we expect everything to happen at the click of a button.   We want to be patient, but we're constantly being pulled into "on demand" behaviors.   It seems we're caught in a perennial tug-of-war.

My 13 year-old daughter recently told me that she is a good student because she is able to "multi-task."   I had to pause to think on this for a moment.   I realized that we've passed our race-against-time culture on to our youth. Except that now it's no longer enough to be doing one thing in a hurry, we have to be accomplishing several tasks simultaneously!

This can't be good for children.   Every day we read about adolescent depression and

39

suicides.   If the message wo send as a society is think quick and act quick, we run the risk of seeing even higher rates of suicide and discontent across all generations.   After all, what is suicide but the ultimate "quick fix"? "I don't like the way I feel right now, so..."

I'm a guilty member of the turbo-charged movement.   I like being in fast-moving environments.   We are guiltier of speed-living in America than anywhere else.   In fact, we invented the turbo-charged movement. During an extended trip to Belgium I recall feeling restless because the people seemed so even-paced, so calm, so orderly.   Cars weren't honking, people weren't rushing past each other. I kept waiting for more.   Of what, I don't know, but I kept thinking that a blast of something was needed to inject "life" into the society.

After a while I began to adjust my thinking and expectations. I began to learn to be patient.   There was no need to rush about. The Belgians were not going to change to suit me.

Then I actually started to appreciate the slower pace. It reminded me of growing up in the Caribbean where life was not a rush (and for the most part still isn't). Pedestrians, cars and tramps all cooperated to share the roads. And I never saw an accident during the time I was there.

I've come to realize that most of the good stuff in life "happens" when there's nothing "happening." But we have a hard time appreciating these moments. People can't even walk on the beach nowadays without an iPod to fill their heads with sound. At home, the TV, radio, internet and cell phone compete for our attention. The constant message is that this moment is not enough in and of itself. It needs fixing and filling up.

I've discovered the real secret to "patience," at least in my own life. It's about living fully in the moment as it is.

When I used to practice what I called patience, what I was really doing was quietly waiting for the next interesting thing to happen.   We learn this skill growing up.   We learn how to "patiently" wait our turn.   But this isn't the kind of patience I'm talking about. When being "patient" means just waiting quietly for your next opportunity to do something, that's not living in the moment. That's living in the next moment.

Much of our lives are spent waiting for some elusive next moment.   And when the next moment comes, what do we do?   Do we appreciate and drink it in?   No, not usually. We start waiting for the next moment.

True patience, the kind that fills your life rather than drains it, means having so much appreciation for this moment that you don't think at all about the next one.

So whenever you find yourself waiting for what's next, take a few slow, deep breaths. Look around you.   See whatever there is to see.   Feel the air on your skin and the texture of the chair you're sitting in.   Appreciate the people, plants and animals around you.   Feel their air on your skin and the texture of the chair you're sitting in.   Appreciate the people, plants and animals around you.   Feel their presence.   Remind yourself that there truly is no better moment than this one and there never will be.

Now, in fact, is the only moment there ever is, ever has been, or ever will be. So live in it. Drink it up.   Absorb it.

If you make a practice of living in the moment you'll never find yourself needing to "be patient" again.   Patience will become your way of life.   Not only will you feel better mentally and emotionally, odds are your health will improve too!

I will practice to be patient when I:

_____

_____

_____

_____

_____

_____

Intimacy

Finally, nothing is as special as sharing time
and space with someone you love and who
loves you -- to have intimacy.   This is what
God referred to as Agape love -- that special
oneness, that special bond.   It gives us the
assurance of belongingness.   It gives us a
place where joys and sorrows are shared.
And it creates the calm after the storm of hurt
and pain that says... everything will be all right.

Intimacy is the crucible in which forgiveness
takes place. Intimacy requires having a
special someone you respect, admire, and
love... despite his or her shortfalls or flaws.
It means having a unique soul that you can
communicate with by just a look or a touch. A
person who will pick you up from your valleys
and gleefully share your peaks with you.
Someone who will make you smile in spite of

your tears, and support you through life's most challenging moments just because they love you.   Someone whose mere presence reaffirms your soul.

Intimacy requires a selflessness that leaves us vulnerable.   And many of us are not comfortable being that exposed.   So we settle for superficial love relationships and functional, I'll-scratch-your-back-if-you-scratch-mine, friendships.   But what is life without risk?   What is life without ever experiencing that oneness that can only come from a willingness to be fully known, despite our flaws?

Let's be honest.   We won't all experience perfect and complete intimacy in our lives... But we can reflect on what that kind of intimacy means and orient our lives as much as possible in that direction.   The simple willingness to be an intimate witness to another person's life will greatly increase the likelihood of that kind of partner stepping into our lives.

Remember that intimacy does not belong solely in a man-woman relationship. We can have intimacy with our friends and family members as well.

Many of us are already achieving intimacy, but there are few of us who would not benefit from a little more...

Intimacy is the icing on the cake of a beautiful life.

Relationships that provide me feelings of intimacy are:

_____

_____

_____

_____

_____

_____

_____

_____

_____

_____

_____

_____

Integrity

Integrity is a major challenge for most of us.

What is integrity?   It's doing the right thing
just because it's the right thing to do.   It's not
about seeking praise, avoiding punishment,
hoping someone will return the favor, or
making a good impression.   Integrity is doing
what's right even when no one is looking.

Especially when no one's looking.

I remember having an in-class discussion
about character when I was in college.   What
does it mean to have good character?   The
professor polled the room, tappng different
students for their responses.   I think I fidgeted
in my seat so she pointed at me.   I replied that
I
thought "character" had to do with our integrity.
It was the spinal cord that holds us upright.

After class, one of my classmates thanked me for making the discussion more meaningful.   This memory will remain with me for a lifetime.   I felt proud to have "stirred" the discussion.

Over years, though, my integrity has been called into question for one reason or another.   I've not always been upright in my actions.   Whether consciously or not, I have succumbed to those human failings that can tarnish one's integrity.

It is usually easier for us to question the integrity of others than to look at ourselves. I can easily recall family or friends who have not been truthful and honest.   Some have even convinced themselves that their lack of integrity was to protect someone else from hurt. That's a convenient lie we all tell ourselves at one time or another.

Young Woman Suffering Alone

I left my daughter with my family and came to start a
life with my boyfriend in America.   I had no other
relatives here.   I'd met my boyfriend about a year
ago when he came home to our country for a visit.

When I arrived at the airport I was looking at a
different man.   He was much thinner than I'd ever
seen him.   He'd lost a lot of weight.   But he
explained that he was exercising and eating
healthier and I didn't doubt his explanation.   I
noticed that he was sick a lot and would take many
pills, and he would always talk about dying so I
would always pray for him and take care of him
when he was sick.

Several months later I started feeling very weak
and went to the doctor to have a pregnancy test
done.   The doctor did a complete check up and all
the tests were negative.   She then suggested
doing an HIV test. When I returned for the results, I
sat in shock when I was told that my test was
positive.   I immediately called my boyfriend from
the doctor's office.   As soon as I told him I did an
HIV test, he hung up the phone and I've never seen
or heard from him since.

What's even worse is that once I came to America, I
found out that my boyfriend was a married man

with children   And, he had another girlfriend that
he was still involved with who also had a child by
him.

Living in integrity, I've discovered, is one of
the hardest things for human beings to do.
Why?   Because the short-term rewards
from being dishonest or selfish are so
seductive.   It takes a really high level of
maturity to realize that these selfish
"rewards" are ultimately not worth the price
we have to pay to win them.   True, we can
often "get away" with dishonest acts in the
eyes of others, but the person who always
knows we've been dishonest is ourselves.

In the end, we are our own harshest judges.

To live a truly satisfying life, we need to earn
our own self-respect.   We need to go to bed
each night, knowing that we've acted in a
way that's consistent with our deepest
values.   When we do this, we begin to learn a
glorious thing.   That is, the satisfaction we
get from quietly knowing we've done the right
thing is a greater reward than any of the

short-term benefits we might achieve by
being dishonest.

Integrity turns out to be its own reward.   And
it's a reward more delicious than money, sex,
power and position.   It's a sense of being
right with ourselves, right with God and right
with the entire universe.

Integrity leads to peace of mind, a rare
commodity in this world of moral conflict and
temptation.

Some areas where I have not practiced
Integrity and where I pledge to do better are:

_____

_____

_____

_____

_____

_____

_____

_____

_____

Spirituality

I'll keep this short and sweet. When we learn to love the Creator and we develop a bond of faith in Him, true empowerment is born. As long as we believe we are random biological beings adrift in a meaningless and mechanical universe, we pinch ourselves off from the greatest source of joy, love and fulfillment a human life can know. The Love of God. It's not that God ever abandons us or withdraws His Love (as some have claimed over the years), it's that we abandon God. We draw the shades down on the eternal Light that is always available to us any time we choose to let it in.

There's a text that says, "if God be for us who can be against us?" Those who develop a deep personal bond with the Divine, who feel the Creator in our own hearts, can face any obstacles that life throws at us with confidence and equanimity.

It doesn't even take a lot to start or to even maintain a relationship with the Divine.   Just a prayer or talk each day will do.   An old Greek saying goes, "The Gods ask little but that they be remembered."   And the remembering part isn't for God, it's for us.   God is not some giant egotist with a neurotic need to be constantly remembered and worshipped.   It is us who need the constant refreshment of eternal love we can only get from a relationship with God.

I recently read an article by a Muslim woman who extolled her pleasure in being able to stop five times each day to pray to Allah. She cherished that time and wrote that it is one of the most endearing elements of being a Muslim.

When it comes to prayer I would add one simple piece of advice: don't just focus on yourself, but pray for others also.   We want blessings and prosperity to be a shared experience, not ours alone.

No matter your belief, commit to spending time in quiet communing with the Source of your life each day.   Peace and tranquility flows from this connectedness.   Understand, of course, that each person identifies her/his Source on personal terms: God, Allah, Buddha, Bahaullah.   The name you use isn't important; it's your experience of connection with universal intelligence that matters.

I will declare, express and experience my Spirituality in the following ways:

_____

_____

_____

_____

_____

_____

_____

_____

_____

_____

_____

_____

_____

Thank You

Well, that's it. For now. Thank you for sharing my little Pocket of Coins.   I hope you have found some value in its few short pages. If so, please pass that coin along to someone else, especially someone who's hurting or feeling lonely.

You never know when that coin will come back to you.

This is also a coin to share as part of your book club.   It will provide very stimulating discussions.

Finally, I hope you will practice the processes you've just read about and won't just slip this book onto your bookshelf.   For if you put these principles into action, I am confident your life will expand in ways you can't even imagine.

Love and blessings,

Donna